Spotter's Guide to
BIRDS
OF PREY

Written by
Peter Holden
and
Richard Porter

Illustrated by
Ian Wallace
& David Wright

D1440111

Contents

Edited by
Rick Morris

Designed by
David Bennett

Additional illustrations by
Alan Harris & Trevor Boyer

Maps by
Andy Martin

Additional text by
Geoffrey Abbott

Peter Holden is National Organizer of the Young Ornithologists' Club.

Richard Porter is Head of Species Protection at the Royal Society for the Protection of Birds. He is co-author of *Flight Identification of European Raptors*.

First published in 1981 by
Usborne Publishing Limited
20 Garrick Street, London WC2E 9BJ

The publishers and authors acknowledge their indebtedness to the following books and journals which were consulted for reference or as sources of illustrations:
The Birds of Britain and Europe. H. Heinzel, R.S.R. Fitter & J.L.F. Parslow (Collins); *The Birds of the Western Palearctic, Vol. II.* Edited by S. Cramp & K.E.L. Simmons (Oxford); *British Birds, Vol. 73, pp 239-256.* Edited by J.T.R. Sharrock; *Flight Identification of European Raptors.* R.F. Porter, Ian Willis, Steen Christensen & Bent Pors Nielsen (T. & A.D. Poyser); *Owls of the World.* Edited by J.A. Burton (Peter Lowe).

How to use this book

This book is a guide to all the birds of prey of Britain and Europe. There are two main groups of birds of prey: the raptors and the owls (see pages 4-5 for the differences between them).

The raptors are illustrated on pages 6 - 38, and the owls appear on pages 39 - 48. There are separate pictures of the females (♀ means female) if they are very different from the males (♂ means male). Sometimes the young, or juvenile, birds are shown too, and sometimes the immature bird (fully grown but not yet in adult plumage).

How to see birds of prey

Many birds of prey in Britain are very rare. To see them you must either be lucky or travel to the areas where they live and breed. This can mean special trips to see the Marsh Harrier in the reed-beds of East Anglia, or Red Kites in Wales. The Kestrel, how-ever, is widespread, and Sparrow-hawks and Buzzards can often be seen in the right type of countryside.

The night-hunting owls are harder to see. Try going out to rough pasture at dusk to see Barn Owls. Tawny Owls are commonly heard at night, even in towns. Two owls – the Little Owl and the Short-eared Owl – can be seen hunting during the day. On your next walk, listen out for small birds making a lot of noise – they may well be mobbing a roosting owl. If you find one, don't disturb it.

Each time you spot a bird, tick it off in the small circle next to the bird's illustration.

The **Scorecard** at the back of the book gives a score for each bird that you might see in Britain. Because some of the birds are rare, you can tick them off if you spot them in zoos or on television.

Measuring birds

Raptors

←——Wingspan 120 cm.——→

Wingspan is measured from wingtip to wingtip.

Owls

←—— Length 38 cm. ——→

Length is measured from the tip of the beak to the tip of the tail.

Maps

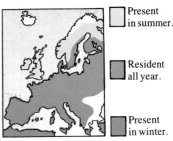

Present in summer.

Resident all year.

Present in winter.

Terms to describe distribution

Resident Occurs throughout the year.
Migrant Visits Europe in summer or moves from one part of Europe to another.
Partial migrant Some members of the species are migrants while others are resident.

Introducing birds of prey

Although many birds eat other animals, the term 'birds of prey' usually refers to those birds equipped for killing with hooked bills and curved claws (called talons). There are two main groups of birds of prey: the raptors (see below) and the owls (see opposite). The group known as raptors includes hawks, falcons, buzzards, eagles, harriers, kites and vultures.

RAPTORS Raptors hunt only by day.

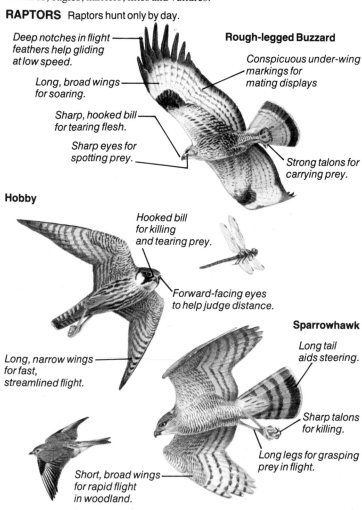

Deep notches in flight feathers help gliding at low speed.

Rough-legged Buzzard

Conspicuous under-wing markings for mating displays

Long, broad wings for soaring.

Sharp, hooked bill for tearing flesh.

Sharp eyes for spotting prey.

Strong talons for carrying prey.

Hobby

Hooked bill for killing and tearing prey.

Forward-facing eyes to help judge distance.

Sparrowhawk

Long tail aids steering.

Long, narrow wings for fast, streamlined flight.

Sharp talons for killing.

Long legs for grasping prey in flight.

Short, broad wings for rapid flight in woodland.

OWLS Most species of owls hunt after sunset.

Long-eared Owl

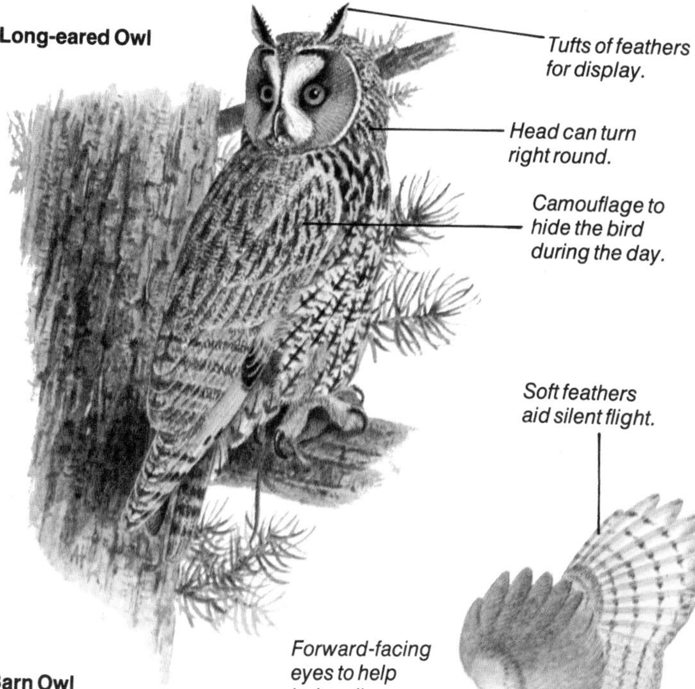

Tufts of feathers for display.

Head can turn right round.

Camouflage to hide the bird during the day.

Soft feathers aid silent flight.

Forward-facing eyes to help judge distance.

Barn Owl

Large eyes to see prey at night.

Facial disc funnels sound to aid hearing.

Hooked bill for tearing prey.

Large ears are used to find prey.

Talons for killing.

Ear

Ears are normally hidden by feathers.

Outer toe can face forwards, or backwards to help grip prey.

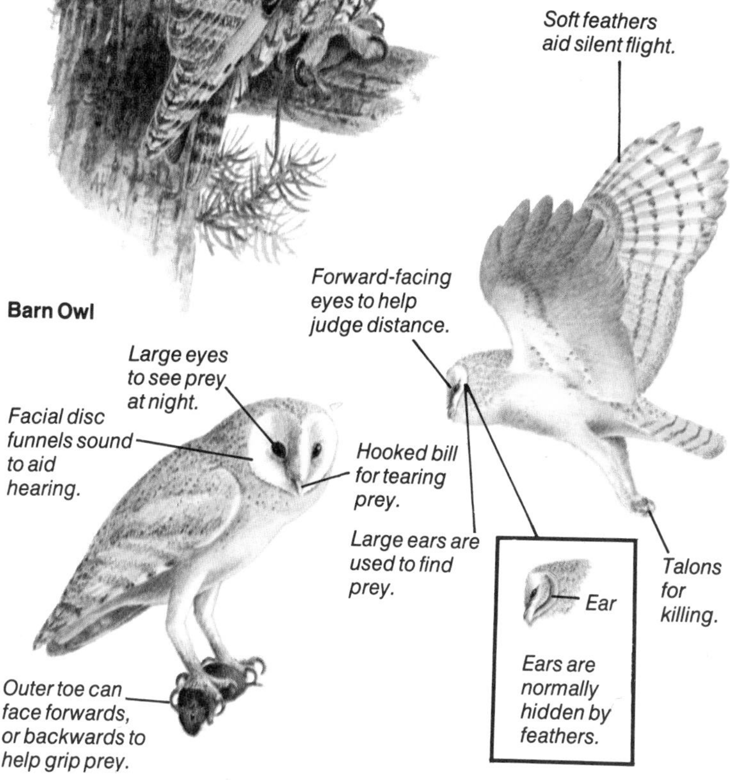

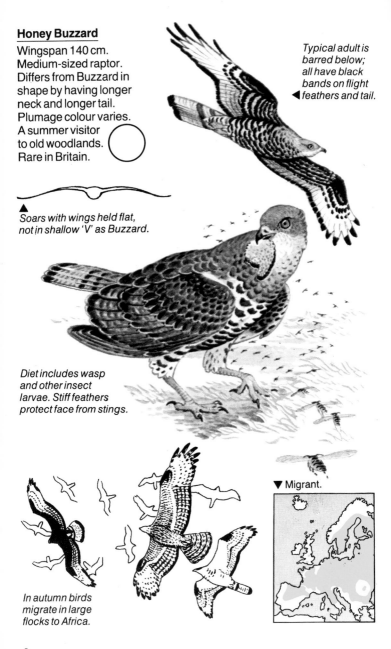

Honey Buzzard

Wingspan 140 cm.
Medium-sized raptor.
Differs from Buzzard in
shape by having longer
neck and longer tail.
Plumage colour varies.
A summer visitor
to old woodlands.
Rare in Britain.

*Typical adult is
barred below;
all have black
bands on flight
◄ feathers and tail.*

▲
*Soars with wings held flat,
not in shallow 'V' as Buzzard.*

*Diet includes wasp
and other insect
larvae. Stiff feathers
protect face from stings.*

▼ Migrant.

*In autumn birds
migrate in large
flocks to Africa.*

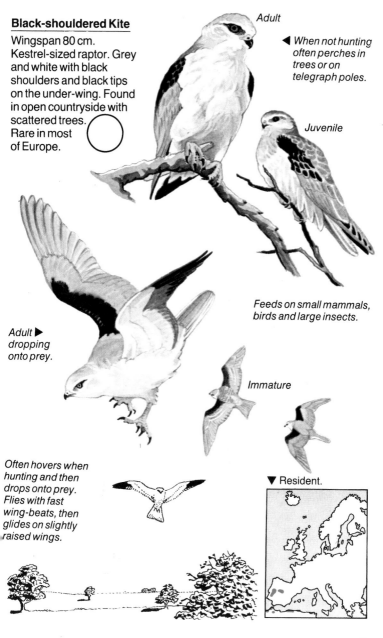

Black-shouldered Kite

Wingspan 80 cm.
Kestrel-sized raptor. Grey
and white with black
shoulders and black tips
on the under-wing. Found
in open countryside with
scattered trees.
Rare in most
of Europe.

Adult

◀ *When not hunting
often perches in
trees or on
telegraph poles.*

Juvenile

*Feeds on small mammals,
birds and large insects.*

Adult ▶
*dropping
onto prey.*

Immature

*Often hovers when
hunting and then
drops onto prey.
Flies with fast
wing-beats, then
glides on slightly
raised wings.*

▼ Resident.

7

Black Kite

Wingspan 170 cm. Larger than Buzzard. Dark brown all over without the rusty colours or white wing patches of Red Kite. Found in varying habitats, from woods to towns, often near water. Feeds on carrion.

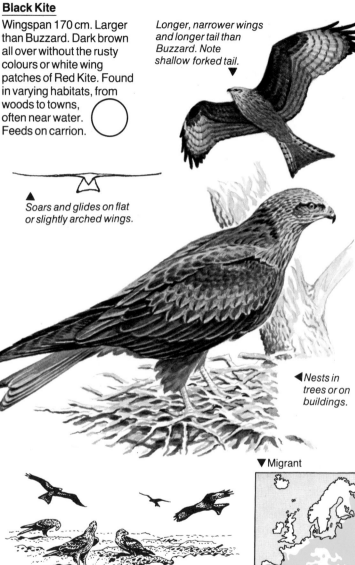

Longer, narrower wings and longer tail than Buzzard. Note shallow forked tail. ▼

▲ *Soars and glides on flat or slightly arched wings.*

◀ *Nests in trees or on buildings.*

▼ Migrant

Groups often visit rubbish tips in built-up areas.

8

Red Kite

Wingspan 185 cm. Graceful bird with long wings, long, deeply forked tail and rich reddish plumage. Very rare in Britain, where several have been illegally poisoned in recent years.

Large white wing patches show up in flight.

Glides for long ▶ distances without moving wings.

Soars and glides on slightly arched wings.

Feeds largely on dead animals, but also kills live creatures including earthworms.

▼Mostly migratory, but resident in Britain.

Red Kites breed in old woodlands.

9

White-tailed Eagle

Wingspan 220 cm. A large, powerful, brown eagle with broad, 'doormat-like' wings, massive bill and short white tail. Likes rocky sea coasts, but also rivers and lakes in eastern Europe.

Adult

Immature

Much persecuted in parts of Europe. It became extinct in Britain where it has now been re-introduced.

▲ *Immature is patchy below and has dark tail.*

▼ Largely resident.

◄ *Adult taking a drake Eider. They feed on fish, waterbirds, mammals and carrion.*

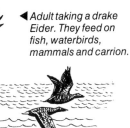

10

Lammergeier or Bearded Vulture

The wingspan of 275 cm. is the largest of any European vulture. Has long, rather pointed wings and diamond-shaped tail. Lives in remote mountains and steep gorges.

'Beard' visible ▶ only at close range.

'Beard'

▲ Adults often have orange-yellow head and underparts but some adults have paler heads.

Adult

Juveniles are darker than adults. ▶

◀ Carrion feeder with habit of dropping bones to crack them to reach the marrow.

▼ Largely resident.

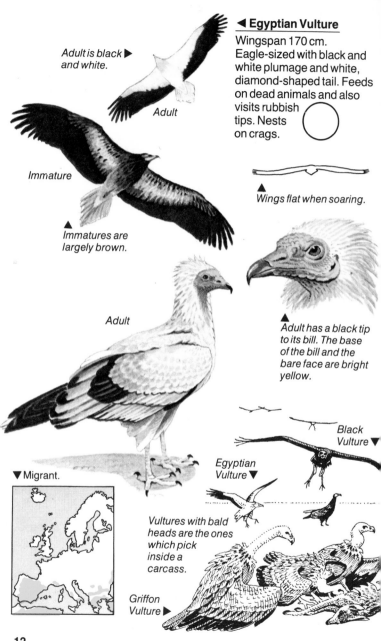

◄ Egyptian Vulture

Wingspan 170 cm. Eagle-sized with black and white plumage and white, diamond-shaped tail. Feeds on dead animals and also visits rubbish tips. Nests on crags.

Adult is black ▶ and white.

Adult

Immature

▲ *Immatures are largely brown.*

▲ *Wings flat when soaring.*

Adult

▲ *Adult has a black tip to its bill. The base of the bill and the bare face are bright yellow.*

Adult

▼ Migrant.

Black Vulture ▼

Egyptian Vulture ▼

Vultures with bald heads are the ones which pick inside a carcass.

Griffon Vulture ▶

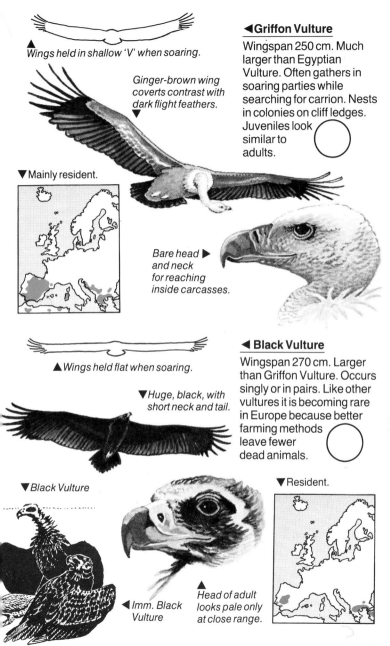

Wings held in shallow 'V' when soaring.

Ginger-brown wing coverts contrast with dark flight feathers. ▼

▼Mainly resident.

Bare head ▶ *and neck for reaching inside carcasses.*

◀Griffon Vulture

Wingspan 250 cm. Much larger than Egyptian Vulture. Often gathers in soaring parties while searching for carrion. Nests in colonies on cliff ledges. Juveniles look similar to adults.

▲*Wings held flat when soaring.*

▼*Huge, black, with short neck and tail.*

▼*Black Vulture*

◀*Imm. Black Vulture*

◀ Black Vulture

Wingspan 270 cm. Larger than Griffon Vulture. Occurs singly or in pairs. Like other vultures it is becoming rare in Europe because better farming methods leave fewer dead animals.

▼Resident.

▲ *Head of adult looks pale only at close range.*

Short-toed Eagle

Wingspan 190 cm. Large pale eagle which often hovers when hunting. Migrates singly or in small parties. Leaves Europe in September and winters in Africa.

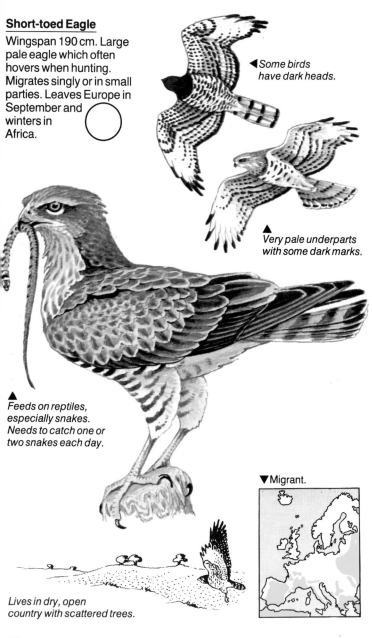

◀ Some birds have dark heads.

▲ Very pale underparts with some dark marks.

▲ Feeds on reptiles, especially snakes. Needs to catch one or two snakes each day.

▼ Migrant.

Lives in dry, open country with scattered trees.

Marsh Harrier

Wingspan 125 cm. Buzzard-sized, but slimmer wings and longer tail. Lives in reedbeds and marshes. Flies with several wing-beats followed by a glide with wings held in shallow 'V'.

◀ Males are grey, brown and chestnut.

♂ ♀

Typical flight path.

▼ Females and juveniles are dark brown, often with yellow on head and wings.

♀

Feeds on birds, voles, frogs and other marshland animals.

♂

♀

During spectacular display flights harriers will sometimes grip talons.

▼ Largely migratory.

15

Hen Harrier

Wingspan 110 cm. Breeds in open country, often on upland moors. Like other harriers, its flight seems lazy with a few wing-beats followed by a glide with wings held in shallow 'V'.

♀

◀ *Female has owl-like face surrounded by a 'ruff' of streaks.*

♀

Heavier and broader wings than Pallid and Montagu's Harriers.

♂

◀ *Male is silver-grey with black wing-ends.*

Male has dark trailing edge to wings.▶

♂

♂

▼ Partial migrant.

♀

Hen Harriers fly low, looking and listening for voles and other prey.

Pallid Harrier ▶

Wingspan 100 cm. Breeds on grasslands and plains in eastern Europe. A lightly built, slim-winged, long-tailed raptor. Feeds on small mammals and birds, also insects and reptiles.

▼ Migrant.

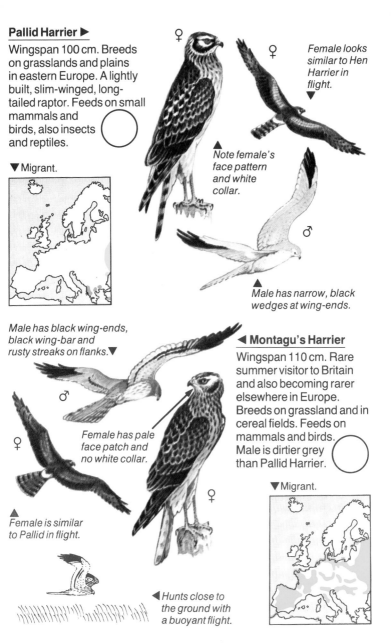

Female looks similar to Hen Harrier in flight. ▼

Note female's face pattern and white collar. ▲

Male has narrow, black wedges at wing-ends. ▲

Male has black wing-ends, black wing-bar and rusty streaks on flanks. ▼

◀ Montagu's Harrier

Wingspan 110 cm. Rare summer visitor to Britain and also becoming rarer elsewhere in Europe. Breeds on grassland and in cereal fields. Feeds on mammals and birds. Male is dirtier grey than Pallid Harrier.

▼ Migrant.

Female has pale face patch and no white collar.

Female is similar to Pallid in flight. ▲

◀ *Hunts close to the ground with a buoyant flight.*

17

Goshawk

Wingspan 150 cm. Like a large, powerful Sparrowhawk. Lives in woodland, hunts in open areas. Young birds are streaked below. Goshawks have a broad white stripe over the eye.

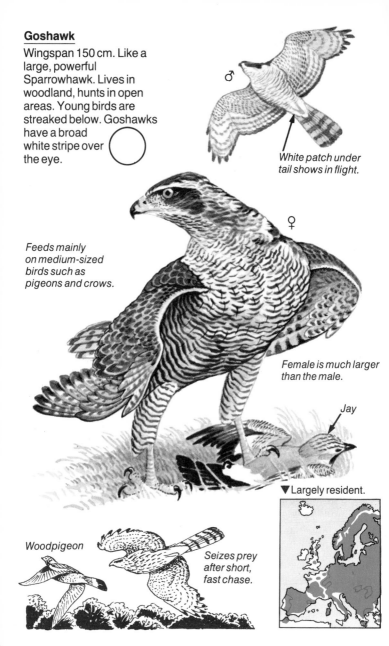

♂

White patch under tail shows in flight.

♀

Feeds mainly on medium-sized birds such as pigeons and crows.

Female is much larger than the male.

Jay

▼ Largely resident.

Woodpigeon

Seizes prey after short, fast chase.

18

Sparrowhawk ▶

Wingspan 60 cm. Male is blue-grey above, barred reddish below. Larger female is brown above with browner barring below. Juvenile has streaked underparts. Hunts small birds in flight.

Woodland bird needing open areas for hunting.

▼ Partial migrant.

♂

♀

Wings are short and ▶ rounded. Tail is long.

Flies with rapid wing-beats and short glides.

◀ Levant Sparrowhawk

Wingspan 70 cm. Female is similar to Sparrowhawk but wingtips are darker and more pointed. Back of male is blue-grey, underparts are white tinged pink. Hunts lizards and large insects.

♂

Male has black wing-tips.

▼ Summer migrant.

♂

♀

Migrates to Africa ▶ in large flocks in September.

Buzzard

Wingspan 120 cm. Smaller than an eagle and one of the most widespread raptors in Europe. Usually seen in hilly areas with woods, open spaces and farmland. Varies from pale to very dark.

Pale form is commonest in northern Europe. ▶

▲ *Often soars with wings raised in shallow 'V'.*

▲ *Typical form. Note brown underparts, paler flight feathers and barred tail.*

Feeds on small mammals, birds, insects, worms and also carrion.

▼ Partial migrant.

Eastern and northern Buzzards migrate to Africa in large flocks in autumn.

20

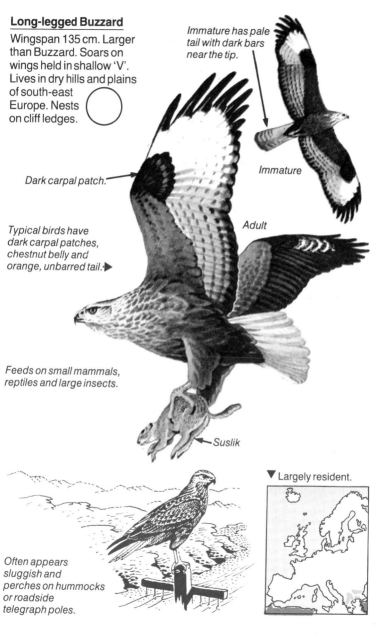

Long-legged Buzzard

Wingspan 135 cm. Larger than Buzzard. Soars on wings held in shallow 'V'. Lives in dry hills and plains of south-east Europe. Nests on cliff ledges.

Immature has pale tail with dark bars near the tip.

Immature

Dark carpal patch.

Adult

Typical birds have dark carpal patches, chestnut belly and orange, unbarred tail.▶

Feeds on small mammals, reptiles and large insects.

Suslik

▼ Largely resident.

Often appears sluggish and perches on hummocks or roadside telegraph poles.

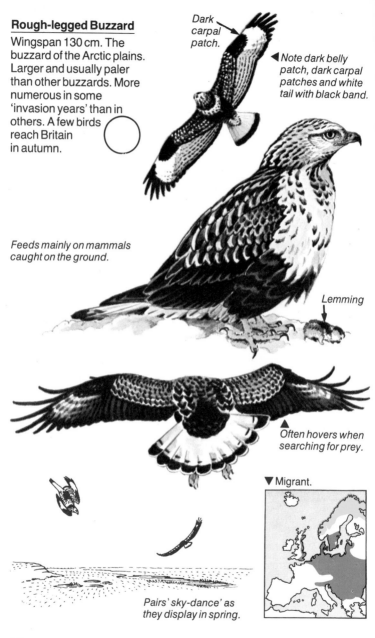

Rough-legged Buzzard

Wingspan 130 cm. The buzzard of the Arctic plains. Larger and usually paler than other buzzards. More numerous in some 'invasion years' than in others. A few birds reach Britain in autumn.

Dark carpal patch.

Note dark belly patch, dark carpal patches and white tail with black band.

Feeds mainly on mammals caught on the ground.

Lemming

Often hovers when searching for prey.

Migrant.

Pairs 'sky-dance' as they display in spring.

Lesser Spotted Eagle ▶

Wingspan 150 cm. An all-brown eagle which breeds in the old forests of eastern Europe. Migrates in large flocks, arriving in March or April and leaving in September.

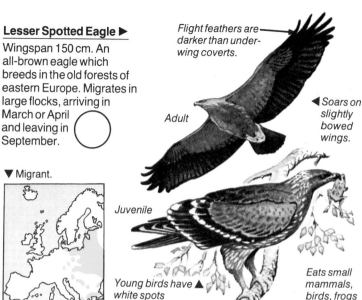

Flight feathers are darker than under-wing coverts.

Adult

◀ *Soars on slightly bowed wings.*

▼ Migrant.

Juvenile

Young birds have ▲ *white spots on their wings.*

Eats small mammals, birds, frogs and snakes.

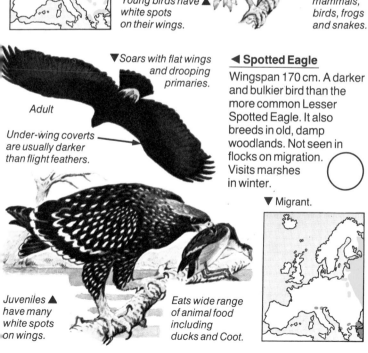

▼*Soars with flat wings and drooping primaries.*

Adult

Under-wing coverts are usually darker than flight feathers.

◀ Spotted Eagle

Wingspan 170 cm. A darker and bulkier bird than the more common Lesser Spotted Eagle. It also breeds in old, damp woodlands. Not seen in flocks on migration. Visits marshes in winter.

▼ Migrant.

Juveniles ▲ *have many white spots on wings.*

Eats wide range of animal food including ducks and Coot.

Imperial Eagle

Wingspan 200 cm. Similar in size to Golden Eagle. A bird of open countryside with scattered trees. Adult identified by white 'braces'. Two different-looking races breed in Europe.

Juvenile is streaked sandy-brown with a pale patch on dark flight feathers.

Eastern race juvenile

Lesser Kestrel

Spanish race adult

Adult being mobbed by male Lesser Kestrel. ▶

'Braces'

Eastern race adult

▼ *Largely resident but immatures may be partial migrants.*

◀ *'Braces' less defined on Eastern race. Only the adult of Spanish race has white leading edge to wings.*

Golden Eagle

Wingspan 210 cm. Large powerful eagle of remote hillsides and mountains. Feeds on medium-sized mammals such as hares, birds such as grouse, and carrion such as dead lambs.

Juvenile has white patches on the wings and tail. ▼

Juvenile

▲
Soars effortlessly on wings raised in a shallow 'V'.

◀ *Adult is dark brown with gold crown and nape.*

Adult

Mountain Hare

Usually only one eaglet is raised to the flying stage from each nest.

▼ Mainly resident.

25

Booted Eagle

Wingspan 110 cm. Two forms are found in Europe: a light phase and a dark phase. Soars and glides on wings held flat unlike rather similar female Marsh Harrier which holds wings in shallow 'V'.

White feathers on legs give this raptor its name.

Soars and glides on flat wings.

Light phase has pale underparts with black flight feathers.

Dark phase is dark brown with pale tail and pale 'wedge' on wings.

▼ Migrant.

Pairs perform spectacular display flights over woods in spring.

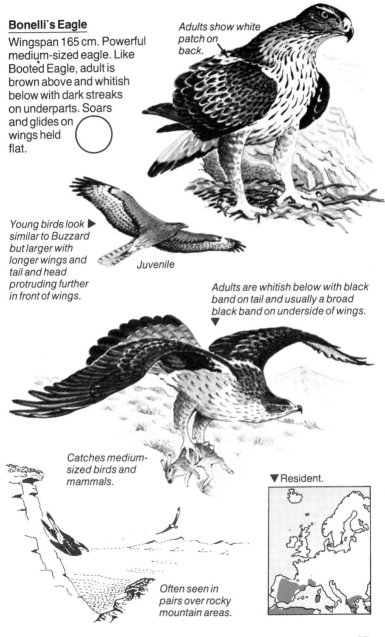

Bonelli's Eagle

Wingspan 165 cm. Powerful medium-sized eagle. Like Booted Eagle, adult is brown above and whitish below with dark streaks on underparts. Soars and glides on wings held flat.

Adults show white patch on back.

Young birds look ▶ similar to Buzzard but larger with longer wings and tail and head protruding further in front of wings.

Juvenile

Adults are whitish below with black band on tail and usually a broad black band on underside of wings. ▼

Catches medium-sized birds and mammals.

Often seen in pairs over rocky mountain areas.

▼ Resident.

27

Lesser Kestrel

Wingspan 65 cm. Nests in colonies, breeding in holes in walls and under eaves. Feeds mainly on flying insects which it catches in flight. Shrill *kit-kit-kit* call draws attention to feeding flocks.

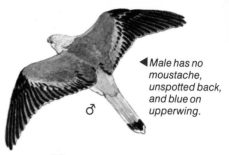

◀ *Male has no moustache, unspotted back, and blue on upperwing.*

Nests are often built in ruined buildings.

◀ *Female is difficult to tell from female Kestrel unless you see her white claws!*

▼ Migrant.

Large feeding parties hunt at dusk.

Kestrel

Wingspan 75 cm. One of our commonest birds of prey, found in open country and in some towns. May be seen hovering beside busy roads. Catches small mammals and insects on the ground.

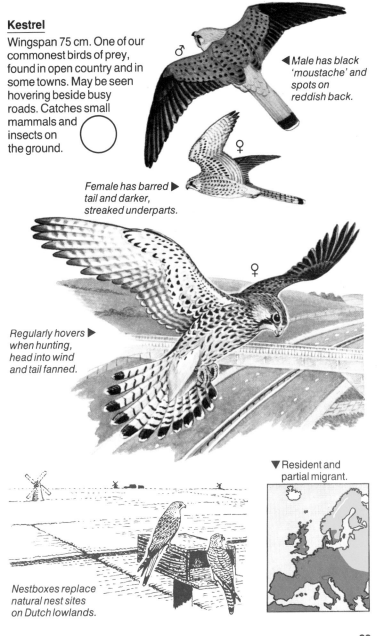

◀ *Male has black 'moustache' and spots on reddish back.*

♂

♀

Female has barred ▶ tail and darker, streaked underparts.

♀

Regularly hovers ▶ when hunting, head into wind and tail fanned.

Nestboxes replace natural nest sites on Dutch lowlands.

▼ Resident and partial migrant.

Red-footed Falcon

Wingspan 70 cm. Similar in size and shape to Hobby. Frequently hovers. Plumage varies depending on age and sex. Breeds in colonies and uses old nests of other birds such as Rooks.

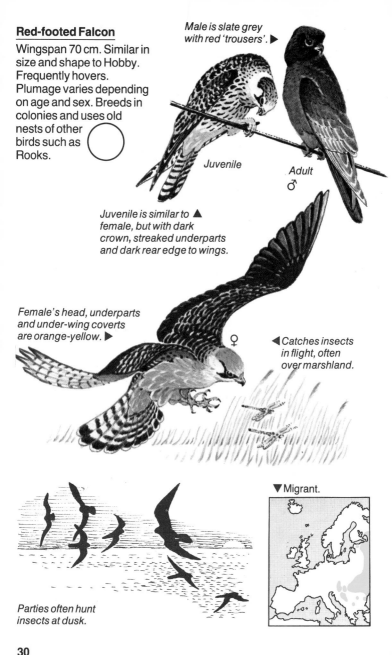

Male is slate grey with red 'trousers'. ▶

Juvenile

Adult
♂

Juvenile is similar to ▲ female, but with dark crown, streaked underparts and dark rear edge to wings.

Female's head, underparts and under-wing coverts are orange-yellow. ▶

♀

◀ *Catches insects in flight, often over marshland.*

▼ *Migrant.*

Parties often hunt insects at dusk.

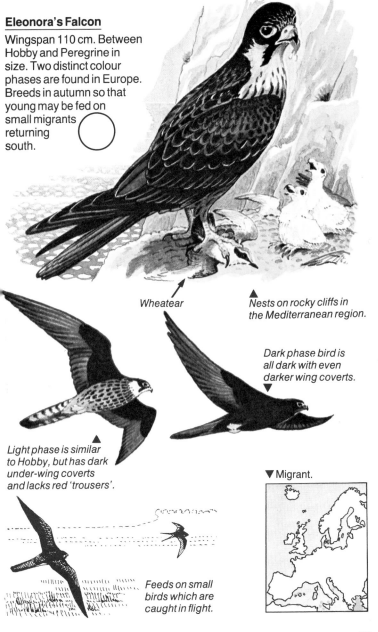

Eleonora's Falcon

Wingspan 110 cm. Between Hobby and Peregrine in size. Two distinct colour phases are found in Europe. Breeds in autumn so that young may be fed on small migrants returning south.

Wheatear

▲ *Nests on rocky cliffs in the Mediterranean region.*

Dark phase bird is all dark with even darker wing coverts. ▼

Light phase is similar to Hobby, but has dark under-wing coverts and lacks red 'trousers'. ▲

Feeds on small birds which are caught in flight.

▼ Migrant.

Merlin

Wingspan 55 cm. Similar in shape to Kestrel, but with shorter wings. Europe's smallest falcon lives in open country, usually moorland, and moves to coastal marshes in winter. Feeds mainly on small birds.

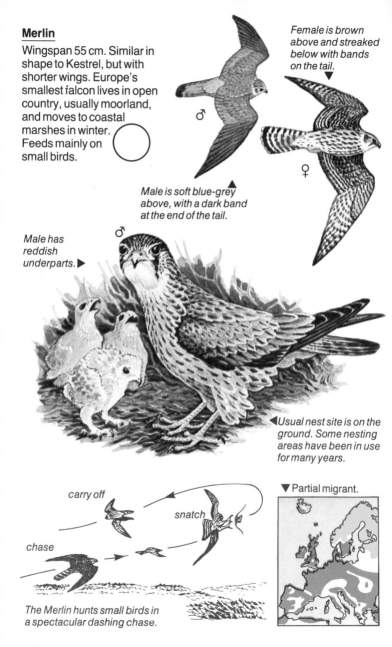

Female is brown above and streaked below with bands on the tail. ▼

Male is soft blue-grey above, with a dark band at the end of the tail. ▲

Male has reddish underparts. ▶

◀ *Usual nest site is on the ground. Some nesting areas have been in use for many years.*

carry off

snatch

chase

▼ Partial migrant.

The Merlin hunts small birds in a spectacular dashing chase.

32

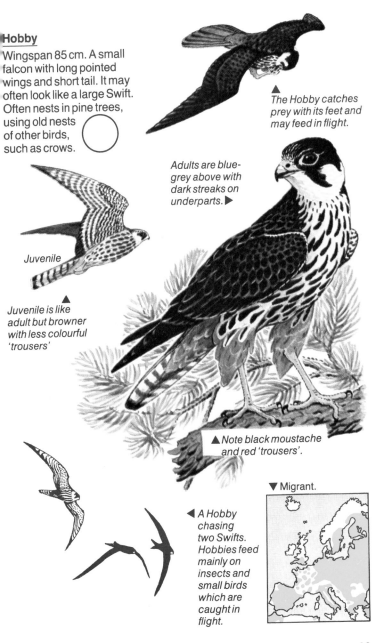

Hobby

Wingspan 85 cm. A small falcon with long pointed wings and short tail. It may often look like a large Swift. Often nests in pine trees, using old nests of other birds, such as crows.

The Hobby catches prey with its feet and may feed in flight.

Adults are blue-grey above with dark streaks on underparts. ▶

Juvenile

▲ Juvenile is like adult but browner with less colourful 'trousers'

▲ Note black moustache and red 'trousers'.

◀ A Hobby chasing two Swifts. Hobbies feed mainly on insects and small birds which are caught in flight.

▼ Migrant.

33

Lanner

Wingspan 110 cm. Large falcon which looks similar to Saker. Back and wings are rather dark brownish-grey. At home in open countryside.

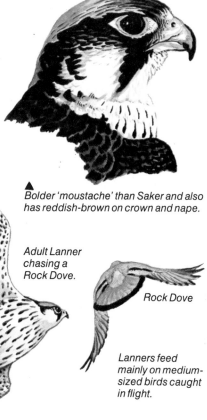

▲
Bolder 'moustache' than Saker and also has reddish-brown on crown and nape.

Pale below ▶ with dark streaks. Wing coverts usually darker spotted than rest of under-wing

Adult Lanner chasing a Rock Dove.

Rock Dove

Lanners feed mainly on medium-sized birds caught in flight.

Lives on rocky slopes or stony plains.

▼ Mainly resident.

34

Saker

Wingspan 110 cm. A large falcon, slightly bigger than Peregrine. Lives on open plains. Upper parts are pale grey-brown, not unlike those of a female Kestrel. Feeds mostly on small mammals.

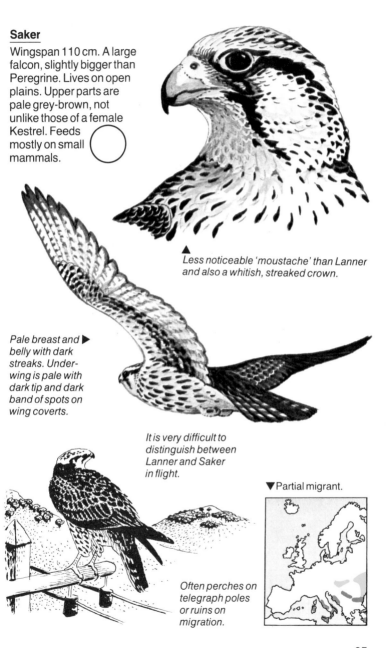

Less noticeable 'moustache' than Lanner and also a whitish, streaked crown.

Pale breast and ▶ belly with dark streaks. Under-wing is pale with dark tip and dark band of spots on wing coverts.

It is very difficult to distinguish between Lanner and Saker in flight.

▼ Partial migrant.

Often perches on telegraph poles or ruins on migration.

Gyrfalcon

Wingspan 150 cm. This fast and powerful bird is the largest falcon in Europe. It lives on northern, rocky plains and rarely comes south. There are three forms: dark, grey, and white.

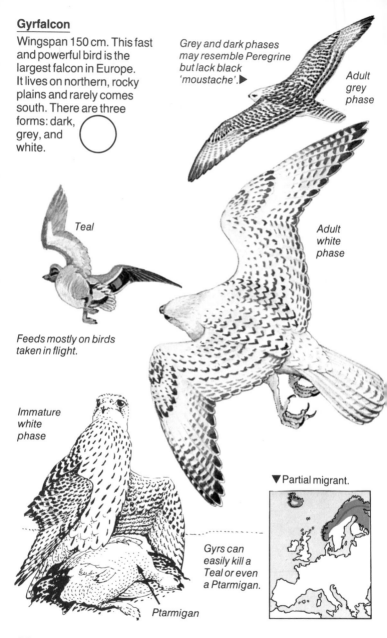

Grey and dark phases may resemble Peregrine but lack black 'moustache'.▶

Adult grey phase

Adult white phase

Teal

Feeds mostly on birds taken in flight.

Immature white phase

▼Partial migrant.

Gyrs can easily kill a Teal or even a Ptarmigan.

Ptarmigan

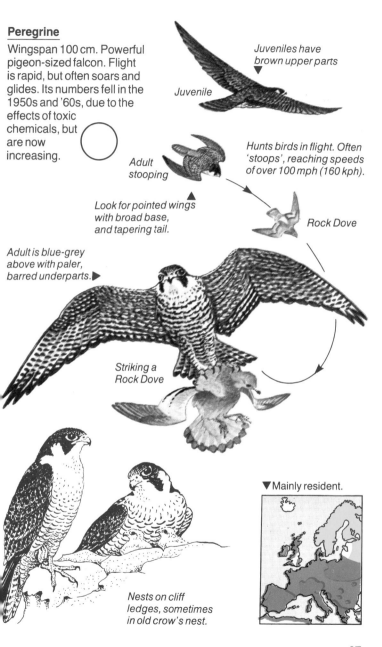

Peregrine

Wingspan 100 cm. Powerful pigeon-sized falcon. Flight is rapid, but often soars and glides. Its numbers fell in the 1950s and '60s, due to the effects of toxic chemicals, but are now increasing.

Juveniles have brown upper parts

Juvenile

Adult stooping

Hunts birds in flight. Often 'stoops', reaching speeds of over 100 mph (160 kph).

Look for pointed wings with broad base, and tapering tail.

Rock Dove

Adult is blue-grey above with paler, barred underparts.

Striking a Rock Dove

Nests on cliff ledges, sometimes in old crow's nest.

▼Mainly resident.

Osprey

Wingspan 150 cm. The only European raptor to feed mainly on fish. Persecuted to extinction in Britain, but now breeding again in Scotland under close protection.
It spends the winter in Africa.

Eagle-size, with long, narrow, angled wings. ▶

Note brown upper parts, and white underparts with dark wing patches.
▼

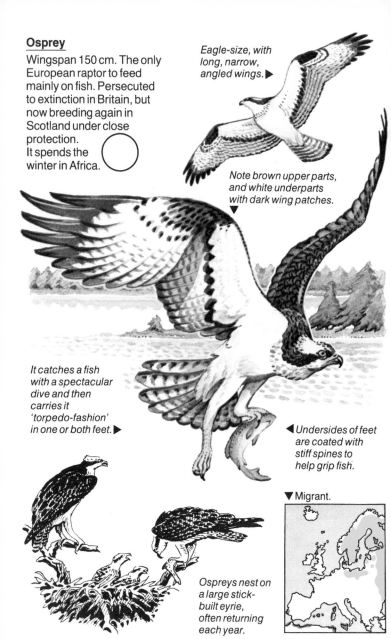

It catches a fish with a spectacular dive and then carries it 'torpedo-fashion' in one or both feet. ▶

◀ *Undersides of feet are coated with stiff spines to help grip fish.*

▼ Migrant.

Ospreys nest on a large stick-built eyrie, often returning each year.

38

Barn Owl

Length 34 cm. A night hunter with a monkey-like face. Its call is an eerie screech. Usually lives on farmland, requiring open country to hunt in. Flight when hunting is low and wavering.

◀ In Britain Barn Owls have honey-brown backs and white underparts.

Feeds on small mammals and birds.

▲ Continental birds have brown breasts.

Often nests in barns, ▶ old buildings or holes in trees.

▼ Resident.

Flight is almost silent.

Eagle Owl

Length 70 cm. This large powerful owl lives in dense forests or craggy mountain areas. It will not tolerate other birds of prey nesting in its territory. Call is a deep *oo-oo-oo*.

Ear-tufts not visible in flight.

Hunts mainly mammals and birds. Large prey, up to the size of Roe Deer, may be taken.

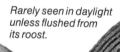

Rarely seen in daylight unless flushed from its roost.

▼ Largely resident.

◄ *Sometimes seen at dusk, silhouetted against the sky, tail cocked and calling.*

Snowy Owl

Length 60 cm.
Unmistakeable large white owl of the high arctic plains. Active during daylight. Often sits on post or rock in the open. Rare visitor to British mainland.

♂

Feeds on mammals and birds. In northern Europe feeds regularly on Lemmings.

◄ *Female is larger and browner than male.*

♀

▼ Partial migrant.

Young hatch at intervals. In years when food is short only the eldest survives.

41

Hawk Owl

Length 38 cm. Found in the conifer forests of northern Europe and moves into central Europe in winter. Call is a shrill *ki-ki-ki*. Feeds on small mammals and birds.

Often perches in the tops of trees. ▶

▲
Note finely barred under- parts and a black border to pale facial discs.

Short, pointed wings and long tail in flight. ▶

▼ Partial migrant.

◀ *Looks hawk-like in flight. Often hunts in daylight.*

Little Owl ▶

Length 22 cm. Small owl often seen in daylight perched on roadside telegraph pole or branch. Introduced into Britain in the last century. Bobs and bows when curious.

Feeds on small mammals, insects and earthworms.

▼ Resident.

◀ *Flight is bounding, usually close to the ground.*

◀ *Has short, white 'eyebrows'.*

◀ Pygmy Owl

Length 16 cm. Smallest European owl and is even smaller than a Starling. Feeds on small mammals and birds, sometimes catching birds in flight. Call is a soft *whee-whee-whee*.

▼ Mainly resident.

Hunts and flies mainly at night.

◀ *Often seen cocking its tail like a Wren. Lives in conifer woods.*

Tawny Owl

Length 38 cm. This is the common brown owl of Europe. Hunts at night, but may be mobbed by smaller birds in daytime. Hooting song is well known, but also makes loud *kee-wick* call.

Often nests ▶ in holes in trees.

Feeds on small mammals such as voles and mice, and on birds, frogs, etc.

Note rounded wings and short tail.
▼

Tawny Owls are medium-sized owls, mottled brown or grey.

▼Resident.

Some Tawny Owls ▶ now live in towns and cities.

44

Ural Owl ▶

Length 61 cm. Like a large, pale Tawny Owl, but with a longer tail. A night-hunting owl of large or small woods. All-black eyes are smaller than Tawny Owl's. Call is a barking *wow-wow-wow*.

Large, pale facial disc.

▼ Resident.

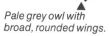

Pale grey owl with broad, rounded wings.

◀ Nests in holes in trees.

◀ Great Grey Owl

Length 69 cm. Only the Eagle Owl is larger. Lives in dense conifer forests. Call is deep *hu-hu-hoo*. Hunts by day as well as at night. Feeds on mammals.

Broad, rounded wings.

▼ Mainly resident.

▲ Greyish streaked and mottled plumage, large head and small yellow eyes.

Uses old nests of birds of prey.

45

Long-eared Owl

Length 36 cm. Rarely seen in daylight. A slim owl with long ear-tufts and orange eyes. Call is long, low, drawn out *oo-oo-oo*. Call of young is like noise of gate swinging on unoiled hinges.

◀ *Streaked underparts show in flight but ear-tufts are not visible.*

Some birds from ▶ northern Europe migrate to Britain for the winter.

Groups may roost together in winter. ▶

▼ Partial migrant.

◀ *Has zig-zag display flight. Often nests in thick conifer woods.*

Short-eared Owl

Length 38 cm. Ear-tufts are hard to see. Eats voles and other small mammals. In years when voles are numerous, Short-eared Owls produce large families, and more birds also winter in the British Isles.

Lower breast and belly are whitish.

May be seen hunting over moors, marshes and scrub during daylight.

Tired migrants may be seen on dunes after crossing the sea.

Slow, wavering flight with deep wing-beats.

Often perches on the ground and is less upright than other owls.

▼ Partial migrant.

Often flies close to the ground and hovers briefly.

Tengmalm's Owl ▶

Length 25 cm. A night-hunting owl found mainly in conifer woodlands. Feeds on small mammals and birds.
Call is a rapid *poo-poo-poo*.

◀ *Young birds are deep brown with bold, white 'eyebrows'.*

Adult

Round head and ▶ clearly marked face pattern.

▼ Mainly resident.

◀ *Dark and spotted upper parts, large head and rounded wings.*

◀ *Its plumage blends with tree trunks and branches.*

Rarely seen in flight.

◀ Scops Owl

Length 19 cm. Similar in size to Little Owl, but slimmer and has ear-tufts. Not often seen during the day. At night its *dwoo, dwoo* call is repeated over and over again.

▼ Migrant.

Often heard in southern European towns in summer.

Raptors in flight

Raptors are usually seen in flight, often at a distance. You won't always see the plumage colours but you can tell a lot by the wing and tail shapes and the plumage markings. All birds here have been drawn at ¹⁄₄₀th of their actual size. All, unless otherwise marked, are adults. Four adult eagles look similar so the different juvenile plumages have been shown. Males (♂) and females (♀) have been shown separately where there is a marked difference between sexes.

Vultures

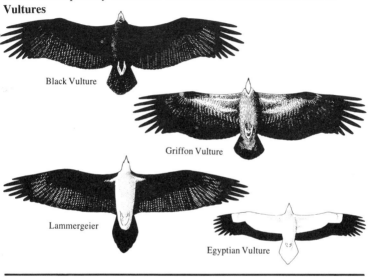

Black Vulture

Griffon Vulture

Lammergeier

Egyptian Vulture

Eagles

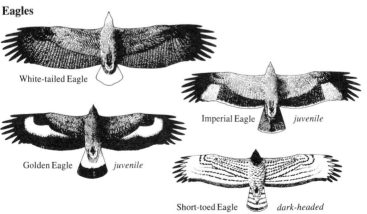

White-tailed Eagle

Imperial Eagle *juvenile*

Golden Eagle *juvenile*

Short-toed Eagle *dark-headed*

Eagles cont.

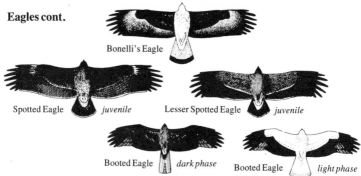

Bonelli's Eagle

Spotted Eagle *juvenile*

Lesser Spotted Eagle *juvenile*

Booted Eagle *dark phase*

Booted Eagle *light phase*

Buzzards

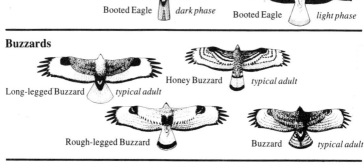

Long-legged Buzzard *typical adult*

Honey Buzzard *typical adult*

Rough-legged Buzzard

Buzzard *typical adult*

Kites

Red Kite

Black-shouldered Kite

Black Kite

Harriers

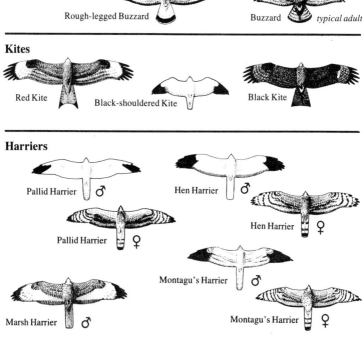

Pallid Harrier ♂

Hen Harrier ♂

Pallid Harrier ♀

Hen Harrier ♀

Marsh Harrier ♂

Montagu's Harrier ♂

Montagu's Harrier ♀

Osprey

Osprey

Hawks

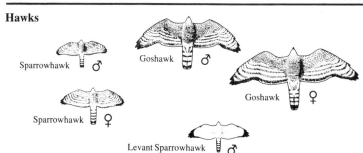

Sparrowhawk ♂

Goshawk ♂

Goshawk ♀

Sparrowhawk ♀

Levant Sparrowhawk ♂

Falcons

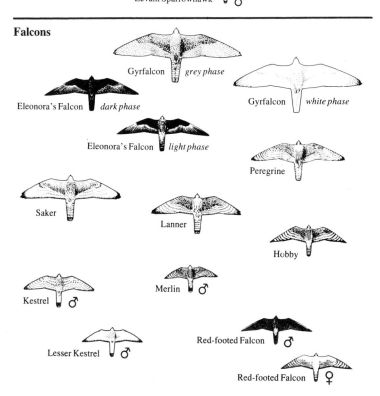

Gyrfalcon *grey phase*

Gyrfalcon *white phase*

Eleonora's Falcon *dark phase*

Eleonora's Falcon *light phase*

Peregrine

Saker

Lanner

Hobby

Kestrel ♂

Merlin ♂

Lesser Kestrel ♂

Red-footed Falcon ♂

Red-footed Falcon ♀

51

Why are birds of prey rare?

▲ Birds of prey are quite rare. Each pair may need a large area in which to catch their prey. Larger species, such as eagles, often only raise one young each year and may not begin to breed until they are five years old. For these reasons, the numbers of birds of prey are easily upset by any form of human interference.

▲ Many of the habitats where birds of prey nest and hunt are being destroyed or changed by farming, forestry, or building. Even in suitable habitats birds may fail to breed because of disturbance from increasing numbers of people – even birdwatchers.

▲ Chemicals are used on crops by farmers and are also discharged as waste products from industries. Some of these chemicals, like the insecticide DDT, are known to have damaging effects on the environment. For example, a number of small animals may feed on crops sprayed with insecticide. If a bird of prey feeds on too many of these animals, the small doses of insecticide may build up in its body and it may be the first to suffer from the effects. It may die, or be prevented from breeding successfully, or lay thin-shelled eggs which break easily.

▲ Birds of prey are heavily persecuted in many areas. This is because they are thought (usually quite wrongly) to harm game or domestic animals. Methods used include:
Shooting
Deliberate destruction of nests and eggs
Trapping
Poisoning: poisoned eggs or small carcasses are put down as bait. Raptors, such as Buzzards, which feed on carrion, are most likely to take poisoned bait.

Shooting was common in the past. ▶
Some birds are still killed to be stuffed
and mounted as specimens. Raptors
and owls are shot for sport in many
parts of Europe.

▲Egg-collecting used to be a
fashionable hobby, and still goes on
today.

▲ Young raptors – especially falcons
– are stolen from the nest for sale or
use by would-be falconers.

Some case histories

White-tailed Eagle Wiped out by
humans earlier this century. Since it is
unlikely to return naturally, an
attempt is being made to re-introduce
it to Scotland with young birds from
arctic Norway.

Osprey Exterminated in Scotland
by keepers, egg-collectors and speci-
men hunters. When a migrant pair
nested in the 1950s, at Loch Garten,
in Scotland, they were closely protected by the RSPB. The pair bred
successfully, and slowly numbers
have increased.

Peregrine Numbers of this bird be-
gan to drop rapidly in the late 1950s.
The cause was found to be chemicals
used on crops. The Peregrine's numbers have begun to increase in coun-
tries where dangerous chemicals are
used less. Young Peregrines are still
stolen from the nest by falconers in
some parts of Britain.

Kestrel This bird is able to live in
man-made habitats. It is commonly
seen hunting along the verges of main
roads, and even breeds successfully
in city centres.

Migration

Migration is the making of regular journeys from one place to another and back again. Many birds of prey migrate in spring and in autumn (as do other birds, some mammals, fish and even insects). In Europe they are usually travelling between a summer breeding area and a wintering area in southern or western Europe or in Africa.

Why migrate?

Migration occurs when food, such as insects and reptiles, is seasonal in the breeding area or becomes hard to find, perhaps due to snow cover. It is food shortages rather than cold weather which cause migration.

Why return?

By returning from their winter quarters to an area with a seasonal food supply, migrants breed better. They may face less competition from other animals which cannot survive the winter. If they travel northwards they will have more daylight in which to hunt and feed their young.

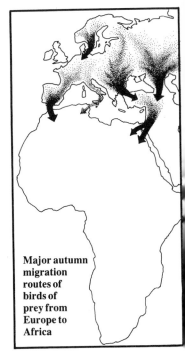

Major autumn migration routes of birds of prey from Europe to Africa

Some migrant birds of prey

Honey Buzzard   Broad-winged, soaring raptors (eagles, buzzards, vultures) spend less energy by using upcurrents of warm air and updraughts over hilly ground. They travel mostly overland and take the shortest sea crossings. Many Honey Buzzards from Europe winter in West Africa, and take a route across the Straits of Gibraltar. These soaring migrants do not normally feed on their journey.

Hobby   Birds of prey using an active flapping flight use more energy, but can follow a more direct route and cross barriers, such as the Mediterranean, on a broad front. The European Hobby population winters entirely in Africa south of the Equator. While migrating these raptors often feed on other small migratory birds, to restore lost energy.

Short-eared Owl   A partial migrant. In winter, birds leave north-east Europe and travel mainly south-west. Many reach areas where the Short-eared Owl is not seen in the summer.

Irruptions, unlike true migration, are irregular movements from the usual range. They are usually caused by changes in the food supply. Snowy Owls, for instance, in years when Lemmings are scarce, irrupt well to the south of their normal wintering range to find enough food.

How do we know?

Leg ring

Ringing a young Kestrel

▲ Much information about bird movement comes from highly organised ringing schemes in which birds are caught and carefully fitted with metal leg rings by trained and licensed ringers. These rings bear a unique number and address. Finding and reporting ringed birds tells us a great deal about the age and movement of the birds.

Wing tag

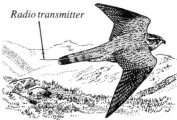

Radio transmitter

▲ Wing tags bearing numbers or letters which can be read with binoculars allow recording without recapture for certain studies.

▲ Following individual birds is possible if a small radio transmitter is attached to the bird. The signal this gives can be tracked by a receiver.

Raptors can be seen migrating at a number of places, and their numbers can be counted.

Hunting

All birds of prey are well equipped as hunters and flesh eaters. They have large, forward-facing eyes to pinpoint prey. The vision of some species is eight times as sharp as human vision. They catch and kill prey with strong, sharp talons (claws). Their hooked beaks are then used for tearing flesh. Different birds hunt in different ways, aiming for certain kinds of prey, so their 'hunting equipment' varies accordingly.

Some hunting methods

▲ The Tawny Owl watches and listens from a perch and then swoops onto prey. Other birds of prey hunt in the same way at times.

▲ Vultures and also the Golden Eagle soar on outstretched wings using up-currents of air. They scan large areas of country, looking for prey.

▲ The Marsh Harrier and also the Barn Owl fly low over the ground, with slow wing-beats and glides, searching to and fro for prey.

▲ The Kestrel hovers, moving wings and tail but keeping the head and eyes quite still to spot small movements on the ground below.

▲ The Sparrowhawk surprises prey by a quick dash from cover.

▲ The Hobby chases and catches prey in the air.

▲ The Peregrine 'stoops' (swoops down) at speed from a height to kill flying birds.

▲ The Osprey dives, feet first, for fish swimming just below the surface of the water.

These different hunting methods require different shaped wings (see pages 4-5 and pages 49-51). The legs and feet vary in shape to deal with different types of prey.

Feet and talons

▲ The Eagle Owl has large, very strong toes and talons for catching, gripping and killing large prey up to the size of foxes.

▲ The Honey Buzzard's feet are used for digging out wasps' and bees' nests. They do not need to have curved talons or a strong grip.

▲ The Sparrowhawk has long slender legs with wide spreading feet. This gives it a longer reach for catching small, agile birds in flight.

▲ The Osprey's feet must catch and grip slippery, wriggling fish. Long, curved talons and sharp spines beneath the toes help to do this.

Pellets

Pellets consist of undigestable food, coughed up through a bird's beak rather than passed as droppings. They usually consist of fur or feathers mixed up with boney remains. These are the parts of the bird's food left in the stomach after the soft parts have been digested.

Pellets are best known to come from birds of prey, but they are also produced by other birds such as gulls, waders and crows, and even small songbirds if they have been feeding on berries or insects.

Some commonly found pellets

about 50 mm.

▲*Tawny Owl* A sausage-shaped pellet. Usually dense greyish fur, showing bones when weathered. Often found below trees.

about 50 mm.

▲*Barn Owl* Often found unweathered on the floors of farm buildings. Usually black. Sometimes has a glossy, varnish-like coating.

about 30 mm.

▲*Kestrel* Found under trees and pylons. Usually slightly flattened with quite pointed ends, and a rather 'felty' look.

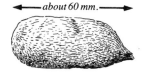

about 60 mm.

▲*Buzzard* Like Tawny Owl pellet but may be smoother (as here). Contains fur or feathers and bits of bone. Can be found where Buzzards roost.

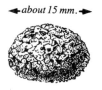

about 15 mm.

▲*Redshank* Small, neat oval pellet, containing small pieces of shells and other food remains. Usually found at high tide roosts.

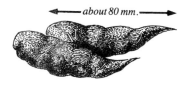

about 80 mm.

▲*Fox droppings* Take care – pellets are not unpleasant to deal with but they could be confused with fox droppings which are!

Equipment required

Dish of water

Disinfectant

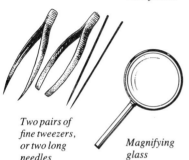

Two pairs of fine tweezers, or two long needles

Magnifying glass

Studying pellets

By dissecting pellets you can very often identify their contents. This gives interesting information about the bird's diet.

1. First soak the pellet in a dish of water. This stops small particles of fur from flying around. A drop of disinfectant may be added to the water as a hygienic measure.

2. Remove the pellet (or dissect it under water if you prefer).

3. Tease it carefully apart using two pairs of tweezers, long needles, or other sharp objects.

4. Clean, dry off and identify the remains you find. You could then mount them with clear glue onto card if you want to keep a permanent record of them.

Identifying the remains

You may be able to recognize the animals eaten by the bird. The most useful bones are the skulls, jaws and teeth, but these may be broken. You will need a reference book to work out which species the bones come from.

You may find whole wing-cases of insects such as beetles, but you will need a low-powered microscope to find the legs and other smaller parts of insects.

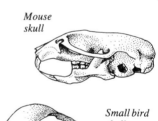

Mouse skull

Small bird skull

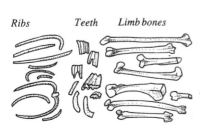

Ribs   *Teeth*   *Limb bones*

Hip bones

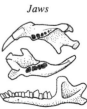

Jaws

Breeding

Size difference

In most birds the male is the same size or slightly larger than the female. In raptors and owls, however, the female is usually larger. Hawks show the biggest difference in size. Female Sparrowhawks weigh almost twice as much as males.

The exact reasons for this are not known. It may allow each of the two birds to feed themselves and the young on different types of prey and therefore avoid competition between them for food. It may make the female safer from her mate, who might take her as prey if she were smaller. It may perhaps help the female defend the nest.

Polygamy

This means having more than one mate at the same time. Male Marsh Harriers and Hen Harriers, in particular, show this. Hen Harrier males have been recorded breeding with as many as six females in one year.

Breeding rate

Larger birds of prey breed slowly. Large eagles may take as much as five to seven years to reach breeding age. They lay a small number of eggs and only a few chicks survive each year. They do, however, generally live longer.

Small species are in more danger from enemies, food shortages and other extremes. On the other hand, they mature quickly. For example, the Sparrowhawk may breed when it is just a year old. Smaller species also lay larger clutches of eggs.

Size of clutch

The number of eggs produced by a female may increase if there is plenty of food about.

The female Goshawk is larger than the male

A Short-eared Owl's clutch is normally four to seven eggs, but in a year when voles are common the number may increase to nine, and as many as 14 have been recorded. There may also be an extra clutch laid in a good year.

Hatching

Birds of prey normally start incubating (keeping the eggs warm so that they can develop) before they have laid the complete clutch. This means that eggs hatch on different dates and the young are different sizes.

For example, a large eagle's chicks may be 3-5 days apart in age. When there is little food about, the youngest and smallest will starve. Therefore little food will have been 'wasted' on them. They may even be eaten by the others.

Short-eared Owl chicks of different ages

Glossary

Carrion - the flesh of a dead animal.
Colour phase - some species have two, or more, quite differently coloured plumages (these are not differences caused by age or sex).
Display – courtship behaviour to attract and keep a mate. Some birds show off their plumage; others put on a 'display' in the air.
Eyrie - the nest of a bird of prey. The term is generally used for the large nests of eagles.
Immature - a young bird which has grown out of its juvenile plumage but is not yet in adult plumage.

Juvenile - a young bird which is in its first full plumage. This plumage is grown while it is in the nest.
Larvae - insects at the stage after hatching from eggs, but before they become full adults.
Phase - see 'Colour phase' (above).
Plumage - all the feathers on a bird.
Stoop - a Peregrine Falcon's dramatic dive at its prey.
Territory - the area defended by a bird, or a pair of birds, for nesting.
Toxic chemicals - poisonous chemicals, see page 52.

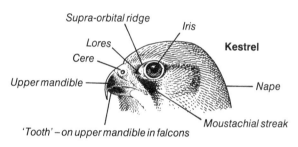

Supra-orbital ridge
Iris
Lores
Kestrel
Cere
Upper mandible
Nape
'Tooth' – on upper mandible in falcons
Moustachial streak

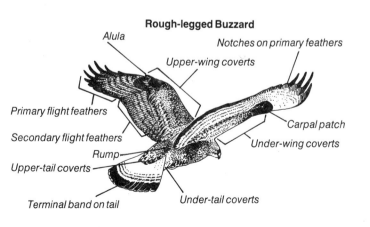

Rough-legged Buzzard
Alula
Notches on primary feathers
Upper-wing coverts
Primary flight feathers
Carpal patch
Secondary flight feathers
Under-wing coverts
Rump
Upper-tail coverts
Terminal band on tail
Under-tail coverts

Scientific names

Scorecard for British species

The birds are in alphabetical order. When you go spotting, put the date at the top of a blank column and, in the same column, fill in the score for each bird you see. Score 25 for any bird not on this list. Rare migrants occur in Britain and you may well see other raptors or owls if you visit Europe.

Species (name of bird)	Score	Date	Date	Date	Species (name of bird)	Score	Date	Date	Date
Buzzard	10				Kite, Red	20			
Buzzard, Honey	25				Merlin	15			
Buzzard, Rough-legged	25				Osprey	20			
Eagle, Golden	20				Owl, Barn	10			
Eagle, White-tailed	25				Owl, Little	10			
Goshawk	25				Owl, Long-eared	15			
Harrier, Hen	15				Owl, Short-eared	15			
Harrier, Marsh	20				Owl, Snowy	25			
Harrier, Montagu's	25				Owl, Tawny	5			
Hobby	20				Peregrine	20			
Kestrel	5				Sparrowhawk	10			
Total					Total				
					Grand Total				

Index

Page numbers referring to main text and illustrations appear in **bold type**

The Birdwatchers' Code

1. The welfare of the birds must come first.
2. Habitat must be protected.
3. Keep disturbance to birds and their habitats to a minimum.
4. When you find a rare bird think carefully about whom you should tell.
5. Do not harass rare migrants.
6. Abide by the Bird Protection Acts at all times.
7. Respect the rights of landowners.
8. Respect the rights of other people in the countryside.
9. Make your records available to the local bird recorder.
10. Behave abroad as you would when birdwatching at home.

Remember All birds of prey are protected by law in Britain. It is an offence to kill them, take them, or to take their eggs. In most cases it is also an offence to disturb them while they are nesting.